Beyond "just okay"

by Susan Padron

A companion workbook to
We don't do "just okay" anymore

Published by

Read
Furiously

Read Often. Read Well.

Published by Read Furiously. First Edition - Trenton, NJ.

ISBN: 979-8-9861199-5-3

Workbook
Self Help
Fashion

For more information on *Beyond Just Okay* or Read Furiously, please visit readfuriously.com. For inquiries, please contact info@readfuriously.com.

Edited by Samantha Atzeni
Layout by Adam Wilson

Read: [v] The act of interpreting and understanding language, symbols, and the written word.

Furiously: [adv] To do something with excitement and passion.

Read Often. Read Well.
Read Furiously

Hi Love!

I'm so thrilled that you're doing this for yourself. You're here, which means that you're ready to dive deeper into your personal style. Prior to starting this workbook, you probably felt like you don't have a style. You can see it in other people, but curating something for yourself feels overwhelming and exhausting.

Whether shopping is challenging or easy for you, a commonality that I've seen is that you can still lack a cohesive style. Did you realize that? Even people who shop all the time can lack a personal style. You can have closets filled with clothes, and none of them can reflect who you are. We're going beyond "Does it fit? Ok, I'll buy it."

Your closet could be packed with pieces that you felt obligated to purchase, because of the beliefs you've absorbed over the years. The clothes could represent a former version of yourself that no longer represents who you are now.

Going through every single clothing item that you own is a very vulnerable experience. It's like you're confronting the past versions of yourself, and deciding who gets to stay, and who should have left a long time ago.

The reason that you're here is because you're craving the connection between yourself and your style. When you have that connection, it allows you to relate to people differently. Allow this workbook to be your guide, so that you don't have to struggle through the overwhelm and confusion.

The exercises are meant to be completed in order, with some of them being limited to one exercise per day. However, when you get to the section on "Burning Down (and rebuilding) Beliefs," you may be in the flow to tackle several or all of those questions at once, and that's totally okay. For all of the exercises in this book, they are meant to be completed with intention. Create space for yourself to think, pause, breathe, and answer. Respect the time you're giving yourself to work through this journey. Lastly, I want you to observe your feelings that come up while you're answering these questions. Observe them without judgment, just let them be. You can process them when you're ready.

Susan Padron

Fashion can be a very powerful tool. Don't underestimate it, and don't sell yourself short.

Burning Down (and rebuilding) Beliefs

Our thoughts/beliefs about style come from all different sources throughout our lives. However, we rarely take the time to question them. Without challenging these ideas, we stay stuck, and unknowingly prevent ourselves from moving forward with our self expression.

Answer the questions in this section with a "rapid fire" approach. Read the prompt or question, and write down immediately what comes to mind.

Don't second guess it or doubt it, just write, and once you pause, go on to the next question. Allowing your pen to connect with paper before your mind has the chance to question what you're writing. Once you've completed this section, then go back and reflect on what you wrote.

Exercise

1

What were you taught about style? List any "style rules" that you learned or that come to mind.

_____

_____

_____

_____

_____

_____

_____

_____

_____

What does a professional person look like? What do they wear?

_____

_____

_____

_____

_____

_____

_____

_____

_____

_____

_____

_____

_____

_____

_____

Sometimes, we have certain expectations put upon us for how we should dress based on our roles. For example, what comes to mind when you think of how a parent should dress?

"I'm too old to wear that." "That looks like something my mom would wear." "No one over the age of 25 should wear that." All of these thoughts are rooted in ageism, and I have no tolerance for it, so let's do some unpacking, shall we?

What comes to mind immediately when you think of how someone dresses in their teens and 20's?

_____

_____

_____

_____

_____

_____

_____

_____

_____

_____

_____

_____

_____

_____

_____

How did I dress in my...

Thirties

Forties

How did I dress in my...

Fifties

Sixties and on...

What do bold hair colors/styles, piercings, and tattoos say about a person?

Does your sexuality or your gender dictate how you should dress? Are there expectations or limitations that exist here?

You have the power and the control to show off as much of yourself as you feel comfortable doing.

How do we translate our personality to our style? Start by describing yourself in three words.

Now remove any words that are the "roles" in your life. Add additional words until you have at least 3 that describe just you.

2

Describe an outfit that you have worn at any time in your life that made you feel like you could take on the fucking world. Whatever life threw at you, you were ready. Visualize the outfit from top to bottom, and write down every detail you can remember. If you've never felt this way, describe your dream outfit that could create this feeling

Diagram your ideal
power outfit

You need your clothes in your closet to support you and help you, not work against you.

Take a breath.

...

Now take another one.

...

You're about to tear down some walls
that helped you to fly under the radar
while staying in your comfort zone.

Impostor Syndrome

Impostor Syndrome prevents you from taking risks, doing things outside of your comfort zone, and pushing yourself to try something new. It's our mind's way of trying to protect us from the unknown. Impostor Syndrome sneaks into our thoughts with our personal style any time you see something and say to yourself, "Oh I could never wear that!" or "Can you imagine if I wore that to work? Everyone would think 'who are they to wear something like that?'"

How does Impostor Syndrome come up for you when you're choosing what you would like to wear?

Does it also come up for you when you're shopping?

_____

_____

_____

_____

_____

_____

_____

_____

_____

_____

_____

_____

_____

_____

How does Imposter Syndrome affect other aspects of your life (i.e. when you're afraid to fully be yourself, it limits your ability to go for what you really want in life)?

_____

_____

_____

_____

_____

_____

_____

_____

_____

_____

_____

_____

_____

_____

_____

_____

Final Thoughts: Go Shopping.

But don't just buy the same shit you always do. The real part of this exercise is that I want you to go shopping and buy at least one thing that caught your eye **AND** is *different* from anything else you currently own. Click "add to cart," and don't talk yourself out of it. (Check the return policy just in case.)

As soon as it arrives, try it on with something that you know you already like (consider this to be your "safe space" item). Also, if you normally style your hair or wear makeup, take a minute to fix yourself up a little. Put shoes on that you think you would like with this outfit. NOW take a look at your gorgeous self. Just like I told you in the beginning of this book, observe the feelings that come up for you. You may not like how you look in this new piece, and that's absolutely ok. Return it or exchange it. My feelings won't be hurt, and you can carry on living your life. The other equally possible outcome is that you do love it. And that's exciting. Why? Because you gave yourself the incredible gift of trying something new in a safe space that you created for yourself. That's huge.

This is not a "one and done" situation here, because you're going to do this the next time you shop too. That resistance that you just felt - it probably felt like a mini temper tantrum in your gut? That's even more of a reason that you need to do this. When you feel resistance, and do the work, that's when your growth will happen. Working through the resistance and processing the why behind it will allow you to continue to grow into the person that you've always stopped yourself from becoming.

Go Shopping -
Room for Reflection

Give yourself
permission to make
yourself a priority.

When do you feel like it's easy to make
yourself a priority? When is it challenging?
What are small ways that you can feel like
you're prioritizing yourself every day?

How would you describe yourself
a year ago?

How have you changed during the last year?

Do your clothes support who you are now?

Impulse Shopping

Why do we impulse shop?

- Because of the illusion that it's easy
- As a form of retail therapy (it's not actually helping you feel better in the long term, I promise you)
- We like it in one color, so we grab all of the colors

When do you find yourself guilty of impulse shopping? What are your impulse shopping triggers? Does it happen at a specific store, a certain time of day, when you're feeling a particular emotion?

Body Positive–Body Neutral

Body positivity is not always achievable every day. There are definitely days when you might feel really good about your body, while other days, your relationship might feel more complicated. Instead of striving for body positivity all the time, allow "body neutrality" to become the goal, especially on those extra tough days. What are some statements/mantras/affirmations that you can tell yourself to help you achieve body neutrality?

No matter what your body looks like, when you go through life, you change, and your style changes as a result.

Closet Assessment

Tackling the things in your closet can feel like such a daunting, overwhelming task. It's easy to push it to the bottom of your to-do list, because "yikes." When you go through your closet, you're forced to acknowledge the changes you've experienced, and this task can be emotionally exhausting for a lot of us. Take one section of your closet at a time, and use this chart with the following questions to guide you through it. Go through as many sections of your closet as you can mentally handle at a time. When you start to feel burnt out, step away, and take care of the rest of it at another time. The end goal is for you to like (ideally, love) everything you have in your closet.

HOW TO EDIT YOUR CLOSET

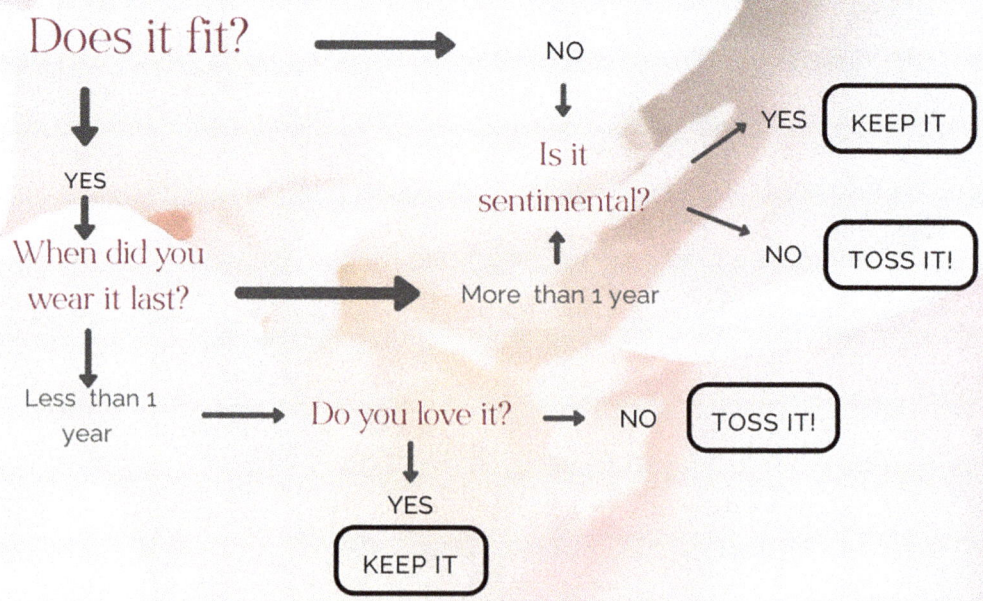

Does it fit? ⟶ NO ↓

Is it sentimental?

↗ YES → KEEP IT

↘ NO → TOSS IT!

↓ YES

When did you wear it last? ⟶ More than 1 year ↑

↓ Less than 1 year

Do you love it? → NO → TOSS IT!

↓ YES

KEEP IT

What feelings or emotions came up for you during the process of going through your closet? Was it easy or difficult? Did you find that you needed to take breaks, or could you just plow through it?

_____

_____

_____

_____

_____

_____

_____

_____

_____

_____

_____

_____

_____

_____

Outfit Versatility

Now that you've gone through your closet, take a look at what's left.

Observe how you feel when you combine pieces with different textures, colors, or patterns. Push yourself to see how versatile your pieces are, and create combinations that you've never tried before.

Style Must Haves

Workhorse pieces: These are also occasionally called "basics" or "staples," meaning that they are worn often because they are versatile and somewhat neutral.

Statement pieces: Statement pieces can be accessories, shoes, outerwear, or clothes. They are usually bold in the way that they stand out from an outfit. They can be a bright color, pattern, sparkly, shiny, textured, or all of the above. It really depends on how you relate to making a statement with your outfit.

Chameleon pieces: A chameleon piece is something that can be worn in many different ways, and it can also work for casual or dressy situations with some easy modifications. Like a chameleon, these pieces just need subtle changes to work with their surroundings.

Workhorse Pieces

Style Must Haves

Statement pieces

Chameleon pieces

Final Thoughts: Closet Assessment

Now that you're familiar with the 3 types of "Style Must Haves," I want you to think about how your style reflects your preferences. What kinds of pieces are left in your closet? Are they mostly workhorse, statement, chameleon, or a combination of the three? When you shop, what kinds of pieces are you attracted to the most? The next time you go to buy something, pause, and ask yourself, "is this a workhorse, chameleon, or a statement?" If you ask yourself that question every time you shop, you'll become much more aware of your style preferences (if you're not already). Answering that question while you shop will also give you more perspective about what might be lacking, and you can encourage yourself to look for different kinds of clothes to add to your closet.

Closet Assessment - Room for Reflection

Being adventurous with your style doesn't just come as a result of wanting to be on trend.

Intuition

Before we approach our final section of the book, I want you to take a moment and acknowledge all of the work that you've done so far. It's exhausting looking inward, and acknowledging all that's been preventing you from being authentically yourself, even if we're having fun playing with clothes. Now that you've done all of that inner work, these next few journal prompts will feel easier to answer.

Intuition: your inner knowing, a gut instinct/feeling

Learning from yourself

How would you describe seeing yourself in the future from someone else's perspective? Describe how you're carrying yourself, your energy, all of the details in your outfit, where you are, where you're going, etc. but all from the perspective of someone else.

When you put something on your body, what makes you immediately say no? Right now, we're focusing just on the fit. Are there certain elements of your outfit that you like to be tight or loose? What parts of your body do you enjoy showing off, and how can your clothes support that? Go through the different parts of an outfit, so that when you try things on, you know what your deal breakers are. Identify your deal breakers, and stop settling.

Create a list of "ideal fit" deal breakers

Tops

_____

_____

_____

_____

_____

Bottoms

_____

_____

_____

_____

_____

Outerwear/Jackets

_____

_____

_____

_____

_____

Shoes

_____

_____

_____

_____

_____

How much in your life has changed over time? More importantly, how much of YOU has changed? Use this page to create a word map where you can outline the roles in your life. What's important to you?

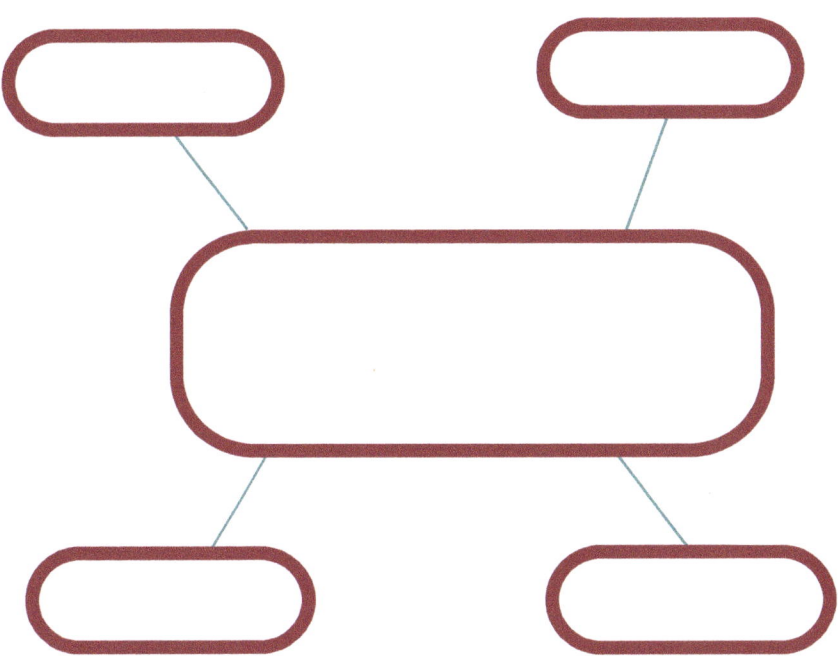

So, how do you end up with a wardrobe filled with only clothes you love? Go through your closet one section at a time, if you don't have the time to tackle it all at one time. Another way is to make a day of it, put it on your schedule and Get. It. Done.

The last option is more of an ongoing approach. When you are getting dressed, and put something on, if you take it off right away, because you don't like the way it looks, don't just hang it back in your closet. Set it aside, so when you have the time, you can add it to your, "it doesn't have to go home, but it can't stay here" collection.

Make a list of clothes that you love

Shadow Side: the emotional part of you that needs work, where you need to dig deep and do the hard stuff.

Acceptance Happens After Forgiveness

Positive Memories

I think it's really important to revisit positive memories that impacted who we are now. It's easy to get caught in a feedback loop of negative memories. We can get stuck, and feel like the trauma keeps happening, even after it's over. But what if we tried to allow ourselves to mentally play in happy memories instead? When was a time in your life that you pleasantly surprised yourself by how brave or strong you were? How did that memory impact you in the future? How did that memory from your past self, high-five your present self and whisper, "you can do this?"

Reflecting on Your Younger Self

Think back to a more playful time in your life - We evolve so much with age and experience, and it's easy to say how we are no longer the person we once were. I mean, stop and think about where you were 5 years ago.

Make a list of lessons learned

Revisit more positive
memories/events
in your life

Affirmations for a rainy day

"I deserve to feel good about what I'm wearing."

"Clothes are meant to fit my body, if they don't fit me, they're not meant for me."

"I am allowed to change. My body is allowed to change. My style is allowed to change."

Use this space to write your own personal affirmations.

Transformation: An evolution, an arrival

We don't do "just okay" anymore.

What are your goals for your future self?

_____

_____

_____

_____

_____

_____

_____

_____

_____

_____

_____

_____

_____

_____

_____

_____

_____

_____

_____

_____

_____

Guided Meditation

Wherever you're currently sitting, while you are working through this book, I want you to sit back, and allow yourself to feel supported by the back of your chair. Close your eyes, place your hands comfortably in your lap, and focus on your breathing. Allow it to be slow, in through your nose and out through your mouth. Feel your breath fill your body. With each inhale, imagine that you're allowing all of the work that you've done so far to integrate into your mind and body. With each exhale, you're releasing what is no longer meant for you. Place one hand on your heart, and one hand on your belly. With each inhale say the phrase to yourself, "I bring in what I need." and with each exhale, "I release what is no longer mine." Repeat this pattern until you feel complete. Come back to this exercise at any time you need to feel grounded, or back in your body.

You and your life
deserve so much
more than "just okay."

Gratitude

It's time to express gratitude to your past, present, and future. It's all part of who you are, especially in your growth journey. Finding ways to say thank you to all of yourself, is how you can give yourself an energetic hug to all parts of you. It helps to create closure and momentum at the same time. Allow it to flow from your thoughts to your page, without judgment of the words you write or the emotions that come forward.

Who I Was

Who I Am

Who I Will Be

Personal Power

Professional Power

Family, Friends, & Support Circles

You did it!

You made it through to the end. Truly, I'm proud of you, and you should absolutely be proud of yourself. A lot of the questions you were encouraged to ask yourself throughout this workbook are not easy to answer, and I want you to release any guilt that you may have if you couldn't answer some of them just yet. You'll come back to those questions when you're ready, and there's nothing wrong with that. There's no concrete timeline for rediscovering yourself or your personal style. Taking the time to go through this workbook, and making yourself a priority is an accomplishment. So, my last task for you in this workbook is that I want you to allow yourself to feel really good about choosing yourself.

Susan Padron

Phases of the Moon
and your style
(@susanpadron_stylist)

New Moon

Reset, set intentions, new beginnings, cleansing, creation, resetting

✓ Set the intention to make time for yourself and your style

✓ Begin removing clothes that you don't love

🤍 I am putting away the energy that no longer serves me and letting go of anything associated with that energy. I AM STANDING MY GROUND.

Waxing Crescent

Nurture yourself and new ideas, refine, strength, healing, creativity, manifestation, confidence in new direction

✓ Allow yourself to find inspiration on your personal style

🤍 I actively use my style to reflect who I am on the inside and represent myself in a way that's true to my soul. I AM MY OWN MUSE.

First Quarter

Reset, set intentions, new beginnings, cleansing, creation, resetting

✓ Set the intention to make time for yourself and your style

✓ Begin removing clothes that you don't love

🤍 With each change and decision I make going forward, I am in control and writing my own destiny. I AM EMPOWERED.

Waxing Gibbous

Trust, energy, strength, renewal, determination, things are happening at the perfect time, remaining open to refining your vision and adjusting as needed

✓ Be patient with yourself. It takes time, emotions will arise, and that's okay.

🤍 I embrace the fact that light and dark must coexist to maintain balance and trust my ability to change. MY ADAPTABILITY IS MY SOURCE OF STRENGTH.

Full Moon

Release, power, psychic ability, celebration, rejuvenation, divination, fully embody your magic and celebrate your progress

✓ Go somewhere in one of your new outfits and take a selfie

✓ Embody your new style and EMBRACE IT

🤎 My inner and outer transformations allow me to show up fully in every space I'm in. I AM RADIANT.

Waning Gibbous

Action, cleansing, protection, gratitude, closure, repelling. Receiving with gratitude, thankful for your blessings and lessons

✓ Purge your closet

🤎 I deserve the best of everything and am willing to work for it. I AM WORTHY.

Last Quarter

Breathe, transition, balance, calming, release, giving back from a place of abundance, release the negative energy and habits that bind you

✓ Donate your old clothes

🤎 I will treat myself the way I deserve to be treated and set that example for the energy of others. I AM SECURE IN MY GIFTS.

Waning Crescent

Banishing, remove negativity, rest, surrender, reflecting with thanks, surrender to the universe and allow yourself to rest

✓ Cleanse your closet to remove any remaining negative energy

✓ Welcome the new positive energy

🤎 I will gladly say, "Thank you, NEXT" to the energy, actions, and people who need to hear it. I AM CENTERED.

GUIDE

 To Do's during that phase

 Affirmation to follow during that phase

SUSAN PADRON
intuitive personal stylist

susanpadronstylist.com
@susanpadron_stylist

Additional Resources

Susan Padron is an intuitive personal stylist. She works with her clients to find a personal style that is a true reflection of who they are as a unique individual, while simultaneously helping them to navigate through their limiting beliefs. Rather than focusing on fashion trends and body types, Susan curates a style for her clients that is accessible, versatile, all while dressing their soul. Her book, *We don't do "just okay" anymore* has earned her the title of "award-winning author." She is also the wardrobe stylist for "Best of Philly's" Youthphoria, which is an organization that provides free gender affirming photoshoots for trans and nonbinary youth in the Greater Philadelphia area.

Susan lives in New Jersey, with her husband, their son (honey bunny), and their "zoo" of adorable animals.

Learn more about Susan's work online at

- susanpadronstylist.com
- instagram.com/susanpadron_stylist
- facebook.com/SusanPadronstylist
- tiktok.com/@susanpadronstylist

Follow her work with Youthphoria at
- https://www.youthphoria.org/

Susan's award winning memoir

Available wherever books are sold.

Find out more at readfuriously.com/okay

www.ingramcontent.com/pod-product-compliance
Lightning Source LLC
Chambersburg PA
CBHW051642120626
46551CB00014B/2181